Jessica Lowery

Spiritual Confidence

International Standard Book Number: 978-1-935920-04-5

Many thanks to:
Bret McCallum
And
Rachelle Mitchell

CONTENTS

CONTENTS

PREFACE

As a cocky young Christian at age 18, I was beginning my spiritual walk with God. Everything was exciting and doable. I couldn't understand the more jaded and worn-down Christians around me. I would ask questions like, "Why aren't more people coming out to Bible study?" and they would look defeated and say, "People just aren't that interested in God." Then my face would break out into a scowl and I would vow to myself that I would never give up trying to make a true difference in our community. I was NOT ever going to lose heart like these Christian friends I knew.

A few years later, however, I began to feel myself wearing down. After a few unanswered prayers, I began to pray less. After trying my hardest to help a few hurting people and seeing them choose against God, I began withdrawing more. After learning deep theology, I became confused about things that were once simple to me. I began experiencing what many Christians experience: a loss of spiritual confidence.

This wasn't all bad. In fact, I believe that God was involved in the breaking down of my self-confidence. But I responded poorly to God's intervention; instead of transferring my confidence from self to Him, I began losing confidence altogether.

God offers special protection and nurturing to many young believers, and after a period of time He lessens the level of nurturing in order to fortify our faith and endurance. Many Christians refer to this period of difficulty as "dissonance," "dark night of the soul," "spiritual depression," or simply "growing pains." During and after a period of time like this, we begin to either sink into despondency or fight for our faith. It is this fight for our faith that we will explore in this booklet.

It's great when we are in an era of passion in our spiritual lives! When spiritual things come naturally we overflow with joy. But for many Christians, a confident spiritual life seems completely out of grasp. We long for boldness, but we aren't sure what needs to change.

PREFACE

I began to study the topic of spiritual confidence a few years ago. Once word got out that I was looking into the subject, I had friends and strangers contacting me in hopes of hearing what I had learned. I put some material together and taught a class at our church and emailed notes out to many people. Even now, I still get emails asking for information. This is what finally motivated me to record some of the studies and notes into a booklet. I know people are hungry for information on this topic.

Jesus said that with faith the size of a mustard seed we can move mountains. Do we really believe this kind of spiritual power is possible? Or like many things do we shrug it off and see it as naïve? Many of us are resigned to live a reasonable spiritual life. We try to think about what is feasible and try not to ask God for things we think are impossible or highly unlikely. As a result we have "a form of godliness," but we deny its power. "How seldom we pray for the unprecedented, let alone the impossible! ... All difficulties are the same size to God." - J. Oswald Sanders

If I'm honest, I'm not confident about many things. If I seem confident, it is often because I'm putting up a front. In reality, I go through times when I wonder if anyone can stand to be around me. I hate hearing myself talk or teach. I feel myself clamming up around people I don't know well. I hear about a friend who is suffering, but I'm not sure what to do or say, so I don't say anything. I even question truths about God. Everywhere I look, I hear secular people claiming to know the secret of becoming more confident. Yet, as Christians, we are right to be suspicious of these self-focused answers. *Self*-confidence isn't biblical, but *spiritual* confidence is within God's will for us.

Spiritual confidence is an *assured spiritual belief resulting in bold spiritual action*. The Bible teaches that this sort of confidence is a good thing. Many of us would love to be less insecure and fearful; and we will see that this is something God wants for us as well.

1

IS CONFIDENCE
A GOOD THING?

Many maturing Christians know that self-confidence is not godly. The Bible confirms this as it speaks out against pride and "confidence in the flesh."[i] In the book of Romans, Paul says: "For I know that nothing good dwells in me, that is, in my flesh; for the willing is present in me, but the doing of the good is not" (Romans 7:18 NASB). So, we may well ask ourselves if confidence is a part of God's plan for us at all. Is confidence good, or is it sinful?

As Christians, we may distrust the concept of self-confidence. Rightly so! But what is the alternative? It can't be weakness; When we look to Jesus as an example, we see someone bold in action, in word, and in belief. We have to know that insecurity and humility are not the same things. Christians can be secure and bold without being prideful.

God is not against confidence; just misplaced confidence. *The object of our confidence makes all the difference.*

Self-confidence is inappropriate because self is unworthy of our confidence. "For who regards you as superior? What do you have that you did not receive? And if you did receive it, why do you boast as if you had not received it?" (1 Corinthians 4:7 NASB). Self is disappointing. The more honest we become, the more we realize that our own devices get us nowhere. Even if we are having success, that success wouldn't be possible without the undeserved blessings we receive from God and others.

In 2 Corinthians 10, Paul writes "For we are not bold to class or compare ourselves with some of those who commend themselves; but when they measure themselves by themselves and compare themselves with themselves, they are without understanding ... for it is not he who commends himself that is approved, but he whom the Lord commends."[ii] When we try to find importance based on ourselves, we have to resort to using unreliable measurements. We tell ourselves that we are doing great - or at least that we are doing fine - or at least that we are doing better than some other people we know. But without God's truth, the pep-talks we give ourselves are hollow. The foolish man built his house on the sand; he lived upon a movable and insecure foundation.

WHAT ABOUT BOASTING?

Boasting is a sin that goes hand in hand with prideful self-confidence, and it is a very distasteful quality. If you boast, you need to have an air of joking in your voice. Nothing cools off a room faster than true boasting.

That's why it is shocking to see that, biblically speaking, boasting is sometimes quite appropriate.

"But may it never be that I would boast, *except in the cross* of our Lord Jesus Christ, through which the world has been crucified to me and I to the world" (Galatians 6:14 NASB, emphasis added).

"And [God] has said to me, 'My grace is sufficient for you, for power is perfected in weakness.' Most gladly, therefore, *I will rather boast about my weaknesses*, so that the power of Christ may dwell in me (2 Corinthians 12:9 NASB, emphasis added).

"But we will not boast beyond our measure, but within the measure of the sphere which God apportioned to us a measure, to reach even as far as you... But HE WHO BOASTS IS TO BOAST IN THE LORD (2 Corinthians 10:13, 17 NASB).

I've wondered about passages like this; what could it mean to boast in the Lord? It may refer to the habit of telling others about what God has done for us. When it talks about boasting "in weakness" and "in the cross of Christ", that could mean that we talk, or boast rather, about what undeserving people we are and how God shows us favor in spite of ourselves. As far as the passage about boasting "within the measure of the sphere which God apportioned to us" – I think this passage must be referring to boasting about ministry. Although, boasting in the Lord means that the joy we share about our ministry is not an egotistical joy, rather a joy in what God has brought us to do.

These passages indicate that it may be appropriate to boast at times. It seems possible from these passages to boast in humility; and to use the audacious tool of boasting to glorify God. There is a time and a place for boasting. In other words, boasting can be beneficial if we boast in the Lord. In the same way, confidence can be beneficial if we are confident in the Lord.

PARRHESIA

Parrhesia[iii] is a Biblical word that is defined as:
- confidence
- boldness
- assurance
- freedom to speak, openness, honesty
- fearlessness, courage, daring
- freedom, liberty
- joyfulness, delight
- a special exercise of faith, unhesitating confidence of faith
- a removal of fear and anxiety due to a removal of guilt

Spiritual confidence, or *parrhesia*, is a concept that is always positive in the Bible. There was a different Greek word to describe the negative idea of prideful confidence. *Tolmao*, most often translated as arrogance, can be translated as bold, confident, brave, or audacious.

Some of the biblical verses on confidence[iv] focus on our belief and faith, while other verses focus on our bravery and bold action.

Here are a few examples: "Therefore let us draw near with *confidence* to the throne of grace, so that we may receive mercy and find grace to help us in time of need" (Hebrews 4:16 NASB, emphasis added). "[Christ] in whom we have *boldness* and *confident* access through faith in Him" (Ephesians 3:12 NASB, emphasis added). "Therefore having such a hope, we use great *boldness* in our speech" (2 Corinthians 3:12 NASB, emphasis added). "[Pray] ... that I may speak *boldly*, as I ought to speak" (Ephesians 6:20b NASB, emphasis added).

We can summarize these ideas by saying that spiritual confidence is an *assured spiritual belief resulting in bold spiritual action*. It is antithetical to the insecurity that plagues most Christians.

When my husband, Ryan, and I were dating, I was pretty insecure about our relationship. I didn't feel safe or sure about anything. He would often talk about his love for me, but I was squirrelly and self-protective. Even on our honeymoon, I remember having a really revealing conversation with Ryan. He asked, "Where do you think we'll be in five years? What do you think we might be doing?" and I replied, "Who knows if we'll even be together in five years?" It's something we joke about now, since we've been married for 12 years. However, the tough cynical nature I was clinging to for protection wasn't really funny at the time.

As Ryan and I grew to know one another more deeply and forgive the shortcomings we saw in one another, I let a lot of my worries go and committed myself more fully to our relationship. Instead of relying on my weak illusions of invulnerability, I decided to let him know and love the real me. And I'm not worried about whether or not he'll be there for me in five years from now.

A relationship with God can follow a similar path. After experience with God and a deepening understanding of His forgiveness, it becomes easier to feel secure and confident. Once our beliefs are stronger, our actions will naturally demonstrate that confidence.

HUMILITY AND CONFIDENCE TOGETHER?

For years now pop psychology has been bombarding us with the message that we need to have good self-esteem. Just watch for the moral of the story in many movies and even cartoons! "Be true to yourself," "Like who you are," "You have to love yourself before you can love anyone else," "Stop worrying about everyone else's needs and take care of yourself." These sentiments are the wisdom of the *kosmos*, or world system. *God wants us to believe in something bigger and better than ourselves.* Rather than self-confidence, He wants us to have spiritual confidence. Simply emulating worldly wisdom and trying to will ourselves into confident people won't work. This is self-confidence, and God wants us to hang our hopes on a better foundation. The wise man built his house upon the rock.

On the other hand, many Christians have a number of misunderstandings about the concept of humility. We often mistake guilt for humility. We often mistake fear for humility. We see being strategic or efficient as a lack of humility. We see being fiery and passionate as a lack of humility. We see having disagreements as a lack of humility. How are we supposed to feel about Jesus fashioning a whip and chasing people out of the temple? Was Jesus not being humble? Or is humility something different than we imagine?

C.S. Lewis described humility as having a "creaturely" outlook. When he was troubled by the doctrine of heavenly rewards, he describes the revelation that helped him understand it as follows:

"When I had thought it over, I saw that this view was scriptural; nothing can eliminate from the parable the divine accolade, 'Well done, thou good and faithful servant.' With that, a good deal of what I had been thinking all my life fell down like a house of cards. I suddenly remembered that no one can enter heaven except as a child; and nothing is so obvious in a child – not in a conceited child, but in a good child – as its great and undisguised pleasure in being praised. Not only in a child, either, but even in a dog or a horse. Apparently what I had mistaken for humility had, all these years, prevented me from understanding what is in fact the humblest, the most childlike, the most creaturely of pleasures – nay, the specific pleasure of the inferior: the pleasure of a beast before men, a child before its father, a pupil before its teacher, a creature before its Creator."[v]

Or, to put it bluntly, "Humility is to make a right estimate of one's self" -Charles Spurgeon[vi]. But, the right estimate is not always negative. Humility isn't always saying. "I'm worthless." Sometimes, humility will cause us to see that we've done well, and we should rejoice that we are pleasing to God.

A perfect passage to summarize the compatibility between humility and spiritual confidence is 2 Corinthians 3:4-6:

Such confidence we have through Christ toward God.
Not that we are adequate in ourselves to consider
anything as coming from ourselves, but our adequacy
is from God, who also made us adequate as servants
of a new covenant, not of the letter but of the Spirit;
for the letter kills, but the Spirit gives life (NASB).

Those of us with a tendency toward pride should note that he writes "not that we are adequate in ourselves." Pride is often a veneer to cover over deep uncertainty. It's confusing when we try to generate a sense of importance from ourselves, because how can we trust it? This passage reveals that we can serve God on a basis other than our own abilities. We are not adequate in ourselves. If we can accept that, it will be so freeing! We won't have to conjure up a grand identity for ourselves, because the life God wants for us requires no such thing.

Those who tend more toward fear and insecurity should note that he writes "[God] made us adequate." We can't use excuses such as "I'm not that relational," "I'm not that dynamic," "I stumble over my words," "I'm not good with people," "I'm not good with book knowledge." God has made us adequate! God thinks that we are all useful and able to do spiritually significant things. We should not use false humility as an excuse to disbelieve what God says He can do!

Our confidence rests in Him, not in ourselves.

2

SLIPPING OFF

It's helpful to think of spiritual confidence as a plateau with steep edges on either side. It is easy to slip off the plateau one way into human-centeredness and self-confidence; and it is equally easy to slip off the other way into super-spirituality. We'll spend time thinking about both of these extremes in this chapter.

HUMAN-CENTEREDNESS

A Christian who is human-centered only looks at the human resources and abilities available and plans accordingly. When we become too human-centered, we begin forgetting about the awesome power of God. Rather than seeing things in a spiritual light, we tend to overanalyze circumstances and react with the quickest, most rational solution possible. Many in this state forget to pray, even about very important decisions, and they tend to experience an inordinate amount of anxiety.

J. C. Brumfield points out, "A life of worry is on the natural plane. The Christian life is on a spiritual plane."[vii] Biblically speaking, worry is sinful and tied up with unbelief. Being in sin means being off-target or outside God's will; and God makes it clear that a life of worry is not the life He wants for us. However, it's easy to see how creating unbiblical expectations and responsibilities would result in worry.

When Moses was worried about his eloquence, God's anger burned and God asked him, "Who made man's mouth?" When Paul was worried about his eloquence, he went ahead and spoke, although it was in "fear and trembling."[viii] Paul was aware of his shortcomings, and felt the stress of being a person with shortcomings, but those thoughts didn't make him shrink back. With the Holy Spirit's help, Paul allowed God to use his flawed mouth. It's natural to be aware of shortcomings in ourselves, but we need to be aware of God's strength as well if we want to think about things fairly.

I'll never forget one time when I had an attack of crying and praying that lasted for four hours. Anyone who knows me knows that it's very rare for me to cry. So, when I do cry, it really stands out in my memory. I was upset and praying to God about this middle school boy named James.

My best friend Jacqui and I had just done some service in the middle school group at our church. At this particular time, I was doing a lot, and now had added middle school work to the list. Jacqui and I served for a week in the middle school summer camp earlier that year, and were just getting back from a winter retreat. I was also leading a few other Bible studies and had just been married the month before. There were so many people, issues and needs flashing around in my brain. I wasn't sure what I should be doing, whom I should be calling, how I should be praying, or where I was failing. But I did know why I was crying; it was because of James.

I had only seen James once. We were at the winter retreat playing a game where all of the students had to throw their shoes in a pile and when the whistle blew, they had to find their shoes and be the first to put them back on. The whistle blew, and a crazy wrestling laughing kid-pile burst into existence. Finally, the first victor emerged! Then second and third place. The energy died back down. That's when I noticed it – a boy sitting near the edge of the mayhem throwing one shoe into the leftover pile and beginning to work on untying his second shoe. The other boys were snickering and pointing at him. I felt that it was up to me to fix this situation, but I wasn't sure what to do. So, I sat down next to him and began untying my shoes too and looking around asked, "Aren't we playing another round?"

That solved the problem for the moment, but James wandered off alone. I asked the older workers about him, and they told me that he doesn't have any mental difficulties. He was neglected by his parents to such a degree that he didn't usually speak or participate in anything social. He had been adopted by a Christian family in our church, but the neglect from his past still moved him around like a silent marionette. I could still cry about this. It became my plan to try and have a meaningful conversation with James. But the retreat ended, and I never got my chance. I never even saw him again.

I think it's right to be moved by human suffering, even to the point of tears. But more was going on with me. I wasn't just crying about James. I was crying because I didn't do much to help him, and I thought I should have. Then I was thinking about all the other hurting people and all the ways I failed to help them. I felt helpless, frustrated, confused, and out of gas.

This feeling has been described by some as "burn-out." Burn-out is another symptom of human-centeredness. It usually means that we have been trying to approach spiritual work in a self-reliant way that has more to do with what we contribute than what God contributes. Sometimes this outlook is called The "Messiah complex" because we are trying to take the Lord's place as Savior. If we feel responsible *to* others, that's a good thing. But, if we're honest, some of us go beyond that and begin feeling responsible *for* others. We think we should be able to change them and if they fail to change, it's because we've failed. But we may be giving ourselves a role that doesn't belong to us.

Recently I was reading an amazing marriage book by Larry

Crabb. It's called "The Marriage Builder", and one of the main points that he hammers home is that we need to understand the difference between desires and goals. He uses a kind of ridiculous example, but it drove the point home. He wrote, "My objective may be that it rain this afternoon...If I perceive my objective of rain as a goal, I will set about to find some way to make it happen; but because I do not have the ability to control whether or not it rains, I will only experience frustration and anger."[ix] Crabb then goes on to point out that we can view rain as a desire, and make a different goal (such as watering the lawn with a sprinkler or hose) that is within our control. He concludes by stating, "The proper response to a desire, then, is prayer. To a goal, the appropriate response is a set of responsible actions. If we confuse our goals and desires, our responses will be wrong."[x]

To many human-centered Christians, we are viewing desires as goals. We need to change our perspective and take a look at which things are within our control, and which things are outside of our control. For example, I may say that it is my goal to lead one person to Christ per year; but that is an inappropriate goal because it isn't just up to me. That is a desire, and I can pray for a desire, but if I make it a goal, it could easily lead to me burning out in flames. However, I could look at the desire and set a more appropriate goal, such as: it is my goal to speak to at least one non-Christian per month.

This attitude can also come out in a different way, in our personal relationship with God. We think if we pray hard enough, read enough, have enough faith, or do enough good deeds we can get God to reciprocate in some way. Conversely, if something is not happening that we think should be happening, we think it's because we need to be doing something differently. But, is this the right way to think about a relationship with God? Paul asked, "Are you so foolish? After beginning with the Spirit, are you now trying to attain your goal by human effort?" (Galatians 3:3 NIV).

I know I'm getting human-centered when I am annoyed by a

Christian brother or sister saying, "You just need to depend more on God." All the frustrations deep within bubble up into an explosive reaction like, "What does that even mean?" or "Just how am I supposed to do that?" I'm frustrated because I want a list of things to do to make things better. I'm hoping to pull myself up by my own bootstraps, and that is human-centered. If we feel discouraged when reading about abstract or mystical ideas in the Bible, this could be a sign that we are in a human-centered mindset.

Provincialism, or limiting focus to one small area, is another symptom of human-centeredness. There is so much need in the world – too much for one person to handle – and it's easier to only think about a manageable area or group. It's easier; but it's not right. Again it comes from measuring human capability and planning accordingly. But, we have the King of this world with us. He wants us to think and pray about things outside our small circle of safety. He wants to expand our worlds, not shrink them. And we should be prepared to serve people even when we least expect it. I'm not saying that it's sinful to have a ministry focus; I'm saying we shouldn't be wearing blinders when we are outside of that arena. For example, if we minister to Somali immigrants, that doesn't mean we should ignore the suburban woman crying on the bus. Or if we have a financial need we're aware of in our own neighborhood, that doesn't mean that we should stop giving money abroad, where we may not know the needs as well.

In the short book 'We Would See Jesus', the authors discuss John 15. They point out that God is the Vine, yet well-meaning people often forget their place as a branch on that Vine. One passage from the book describes it:

> It is possible for any of us at any time to assume the position, often unconsciously, of the vine. We start the day as if it were *our* day and we make *our* plans for *our* day and fully intend to do *our* best for the Lord … The very responsibility of trying to be the vine makes

us tense, and this tenseness always predisposes us to
further sin ... [God] is the Vine to me only as I repent
of trying to be the vine myself (emphasis mine).

In other words, many of us forget the part in the Lord's prayer
that suggests we ask for God's will to be done, and instead we're
running around full of plans and ideas for how God can bless our will
each day. *It would dramatically improve our disposition if we could be
content as a branch*.

"Come now, you who say, "Today or tomorrow we will go
into such a town and spend a year there and trade and make a profit"
– yet you do not know what tomorrow will bring. What is your life?
For you are a mist that appears for a little while and then vanishes.
Instead you ought to say, "If the Lord wills, we will live and do this
or that." –James 4:13-15

The remedy to a human-centered attitude is a growing
appreciation for the sovereign action of God. I've included a short
study of God's providence in Appendix A.

SUPER-SPIRITUALITY

Super-spirituality is a term that isn't used much; it refers to a
Christian who downplays the need for human agency. Human-
centered Christians are too focused on human action and not focused
enough on the providence of God. Super-spiritual Christians have the
opposite problem. When we slip into super-spirituality, we fail to
appreciate the role of human responsibility. Super-Spirituality is a
term coined by Francis Schaeffer in his book "*The New Super-
Spirituality*."[xii] He means this title sarcastically. It is not that Christians
in this category are extra spiritual, but that they use spirituality as an
excuse for being presumptuous.

As super-spiritual Christians, we may talk about grace and the
power of God, but by our undisciplined and narrow lives we show
that we actually do not understand much. If God were half as good

as we say He is, we should be obeying Him, and human responsibility is part of the equation. Oswald Chambers says, "It is the unseen and the spiritual in people that determines the outward and the actual." Our actions, or lack thereof, say something about our spiritual lives.

As Christians we should know what it feels like to be hit by a conviction that we need to act upon. It's like being hit by an arrow, and we need to let it sink in and change us. We should never try to use grace defensively, as a shield to protect us from these arrows of God's truth. We must be convicted, we must act, we must be out on the streets meeting needs, we must be carving out time to spend with our Father and Leader, and we must be lovingly involved with the Body. "For you were called to freedom, brothers. Only do not use your freedom as an opportunity for the flesh, but through love serve one another" (Galatians 5:13 ESV). Grace does free us from the Law, but grace is also supposed to lead us toward holiness.

As a young Christian, I was very super-spiritual. I saw spirituality as an experience for me, and believed that I didn't need to act in my relationships with others. I thought it would be arrogant to think I needed to do anything. If God wanted something done, He would make sure it was done. I remember my Christian friends quoting an Isaiah verse a lot that said something about our righteous deeds being like dirty rags to God. This made perfect sense to me. Why would God, who is so high above us, think anything of our pitiful attempts at goodness?

Later, when my struggles with the idea of human agency came to a head, I spent a year studying the topic. In the first book I read, the authors brought up the very verse in Isaiah that had been quoted to me so many times and refuted it! The verse in Isaiah 64:6 is a complaint prayer. The basic thought is "Why is God viewing our righteous works as dirty rags? Why is he hiding His face from what we're going through?" And God refutes their view of Him in the next section,[xiii] essentially saying, "That is not what's happening!" *God is pleased with us and our work*! Realizing this opened the door for me to see what true humility is, rather than the anemic substitute for humility that I had created. "But the LORD takes pleasure in those who fear Him, in those who hope in His steadfast love" (Psalm 147:11 ESV).

I think the best litmus test that we can give ourselves to know if we struggle with super-spirituality, is that of uncomfortable doctrines. There are a few subjects raised in the Bible which make super-spiritual Christians really uncomfortable. One is the idea of spiritual rewards. Have we ever heard someone talking about rewards in heaven and felt a bit funny about it; wondering if it was somehow selfish or prideful to be motivated by spiritual rewards? If so, it may be an indication that we have some traces of super-spirituality in our minds. We may think that this comes from a place of humility because we don't feel it's right to be rewarded for what we've done. But, most likely it is our super-spiritual force-field and not our humility that motivates us to feel this way.

Remember in chapter one, I mentioned C.S. Lewis' struggle with this very doctrine. He claimed that it was not fashionable, or modern, to believe in something like rewards. Why? Because rewards are either for humble beasts like dogs and horses, or for children. They act well, and receive a pat on the head. And it is the fact that we either do not want to act well, or do not want the pat on the head that causes us to get uncomfortable with this doctrine. We do not squirm because of our humility.

When we are slipping into super-spirituality, we'll also be uncomfortable with the biblical topic of human agency in general. In 1 Corinthians 3:9, Paul says that we are God's co-workers, and in John 4 Jesus claims that people are like fruit to be harvested by Christians. These ideas are very confusing to super-spiritual Believers. It feels wrong; it feels sacrilegious. Isn't that making people into projects? Isn't that arrogant to put us up on the same level as God? But God never wanted us to act as spiritual gluttons, only focused on how to take in as much spirituality as possible. We are meant to be missional; to be conduits of spirituality and love for others. And if God chooses to use me in His mission, who am I to refuse Him?

Finally, the idea that church should be organized and efficient may not sit well if we have traces of super-spirituality within. As rebellious people, it's fun to find issues with the running of the church – but we should keep in mind that efficiency and organization are not intrinsically unspiritual things. When Paul describes orderly church meetings, he concludes: "For [our] God is not a God of confusion but [a God] of peace" (1 Corinthians 14:33 NASB).

Super-spiritual Christians are often more focused on restrictions than on true virtues and action. Some Christians believe that anything enjoyable is probably bad, or unspiritual. I've heard people put it into sentences as plain as, "Well I really want to *blank*, so God must want *opposite blank*." I think this happens a lot. Sometimes it's a good thing, but often we are just trying to find a way to have some easy, albeit self-created, spiritual success. We want to point to the restrictions we keep on ourselves, and ignore the fact that we are not practicing active love. Whereas, the Bible seems to approach things differently, claiming that "love covers a multitude of sins."[xiv]

Other times, when we are slipping into super-spirituality, we may worry too much about our motives. We may even shrink back from good work because we are concerned that there may be something intrinsically unspiritual within us, maybe even something that we don't understand. For example, one young guy talked about how he was doing a lot of evangelism, but it was going to his head. He said that he had decided he wanted to stop talking to anyone for a while to clear his head, then he could get better motives and start reaching out in love again. I wonder if that sort of plan is realistic. Anecdotally, this particular man withdrew from all relationships for a while and then began to self-destruct. But, I don't want to communicate anything dogmatic here, I just want to question that sort of reasoning. Some things are always good to do, whether by good or bad motives. At the end of the list of the fruits of the spirit in Galatians, it claims, "against such things there is no law" (Galatians 5:23b NASB). In other words, there are some things that are never wrong to do. Paul said in Philippians, "Some indeed preach Christ from envy and rivalry, but others from good will ...What then? Only that in every way, whether in pretense or in truth, Christ is proclaimed, and in that I rejoice" (Philippians 1:15, 18 ESV). He also alludes to the fact that he doesn't waste time worrying about his own motives in 1 Corinthians 4. He says he doesn't judge himself in that way, and doesn't care if others judge him in that way; he leaves it to God to eventually show his true motives.

The problem with super-spirituality is that it either denies or downplays the role of human action in spiritual matters. A "let go, let God" attitude is presumptuous and spiritually lazy. It's also unbiblical. According to the Bible, our actions matter and may have eternal implications. We need to see that this doesn't downplay God's sovereignty at all. *It was in his sovereign design to give us some responsibility.* I've included a short study on human agency in the second half of Appendix A.

CONCLUSION

Most people fall into either one or both of these extremes at times. Very few Christians would say that they have a perfectly balanced view of God's sovereign action and human responsibility. It's helpful to think about both extremes and try to understand where we veer off into misunderstanding. This will ultimately help us develop more spiritual confidence. When we can appreciate both the role of God and our own role, we will have a stronger faith relationship with God and a more spiritually bold lifestyle.

GUILT

*"We are of the truth and reassure our heart before Him;
for whenever our heart condemns us, God is greater than
our heart, and He knows everything. Beloved, if our
heart does not condemn us, we have confidence before
God" (1 John 3:19b-21 ESV).*

This verse implies that guilt is directly antithetical to the spiritual
confidence we could be enjoying. Furthermore, this verse makes the
point that God is greater than our hearts and knows everything. God
knows the things we are guilty of, and He accepts us despite those
things. Our knowledge of this acceptance will help us to "reassure our
heart before Him."

Guilt can be a result of satanic attack or it can be something
we manufacture ourselves. We can become mired in guilty feelings.
When we do, it is the opposite of the freedom and confidence that
God went to great lengths to make available to us.

Guilt alone is not necessarily a good thing or a bad thing. It
is a legal term having to do with an evaluation of our actions.
Unfortunately, when we experience guilty thoughts, the emotional
reaction of shame is almost always close behind. Shame is an
alienating and often fatalistic emotion. When we indulge in shame, or
guilty feelings, we often freeze up and feel completely paralyzed. We

feel bad, but instead of being motivated to change, we remain stuck; and a gap of alienation opens wider and wider between us and others. We begin to think of God as a disappointed father, and our estrangement with God becomes stronger and more acute.

Guilt is not humility. Guilt is not spiritual grieving either. When we experience feelings of guilt, it is often because of pride or unbelief. God has forgiven us! But accepting God's forgiveness and letting things go seems too easy. *We are like patients telling the doctor that he has given us the wrong diagnosis.* We know that there are big problems the doctor overlooked. The only problem is that the doctor in this metaphor is our Creator, and we should trust what He says about us. Let's look at some of the things He says about us in the Bible:

> "Therefore, brethren, since we have confidence to enter the holy place by the blood of Jesus ... let us draw near with a sincere heart in full assurance of faith, having our hearts sprinkled clean from an evil conscience and our bodies washed with pure water" (Hebrews 10:19, 22 NASB).
> "I do not nullify the grace of God, for if righteousness comes through the Law, then Christ died needlessly" (Galatians 2:21 *NASB*).
> *"Who will bring a charge against God's elect? God is the one who justifies" (Romans 8:33 NASB).*

When we allow our feelings of guilt to trump the truths we've learned in the Bible, we are disagreeing with God. God is the ultimate Judge and King. We are subject to His declarations. It's easy to think of guilt an innocent and maybe even admirable quality; but, we need to see guilty feelings for what they really are ... areas of unbelief.

When Satan makes his accusations, he is hoping we will become ensnared in guilt feelings. If we feel true conviction from God to change something in our actions or character, we will often have a specific change in mind, whereas satanic accusations are vague and confusing. Conviction from God often leaves us motivated to make a change, whereas satanic accusations leave us hopeless. Conviction from God can be corroborated by other believers, whereas satanic accusations are often denounced when we share them with others. As Thomas a Kempis put it, "You see, one must always get back to the practical and definite. What the devil loves is that vague cloud of unspecified guilt feeling or unspecified virtue by which he lures us into despair or presumption."[xv] At Xenos, we teach a class on recognizing the difference between conviction and accusation, and it can be read online at www.xenos.org.[xvi]

It is dangerous to believe that accusation is actually conviction. If we make that mistake, we are giving credence to the accusations of God's enemy. It's also dangerous to write off true conviction from God, chalking it up to unfounded feelings of guilt we should write off. If we make that mistake, we would breeze past lessons that God may want us to see. It's easy to fall into either error, which is why it is so important to be objective about our guilt.

If we tend toward super-spirituality, we may try to deal with guilt feelings alone, believing that everything can be dealt with between God and ourselves. However, this may cause some residual guilt and alienation to remain. Since guilt and conviction are both working through the conscience, guilt can be a pretty confusing thing. Talking with someone else can bring a lot of clarity. It can also be extremely freeing to experience the grace of God through a Christian friend. Sometimes we believe that if we work things out "between us and God," we don't need to go back to the person we've wronged and seek forgiveness. I think this is ultimately true, however I have never regretted being honest about my wrongs with others.

For example, once after being married for six years, my husband brought up a story that I had told him when we were dating. I felt a flash of embarrassment when he mentioned it, because I realized that the story he was referring to was something I had lied about. I didn't say anything at the moment, because as a story-teller and an exaggerator, I'm always ashamed when I have to discredit myself further by admitting that sometimes I'm untrustworthy. But the thought of it came up occasionally as I was sitting in a teaching or praying or just sitting on the couch. Finally, I had enough! I clumsily approached Ryan and told him the truth. To be honest, he didn't even remember what I was talking about! But we had a good talk and a laugh or two, and it strengthened our relationship. And I really think it was worth it; the peace of mind alone is worth the awkward moment.

The human-centered Christian may try to just shake off guilt feelings without consulting God. Or they may try to get validation from "yes-men" without serious spiritual reflection and development of a conviction. This type of reaction will likely result in the guilt resurfacing. *Spiritual problems require spiritual solutions.*

DEALING WITH GUILT

When our conscience is bothering us, we should prayerfully evaluate the problem. Is the problem we are thinking about something morally wrong that God may be challenging us about? Are we unable to put a finger on anything tangibly wrong? If we conclude that there is an issue, we can repent for that and accept God's grace in that area in our lives. If we conclude that we may be experiencing satanic accusation or baseless shame, we can ask God for freedom in that area. It is good to renounce the thought. Paul describes taking certain thoughts "captive" in second Corinthians 10. In other words, jail the thought, cast it down. When it resurfaces, ask Christ to take it away from your mind again. It is important to replace the thought with a memory verse that applies to the area of struggle.

Many of us assign guilt to the wrong area. When we are upset at ourselves for not relating with someone enough, we may feel bad about our lack of time. We think, "If only I weren't so busy, I would be able to spend more time with so-and-so." However, our lack of time is not the problem. The problem is that we failed to initiate with our friend. Or we may feel guilty when something goes wrong and we say, "If only I had known and seen this coming," when the action we are guilty of is actually prayerlessness. Cornelius Van Til described our failure to assign guilt to the correct area this way:

> In conjunction with man's false ideal of knowledge, we may mention here the fact that when man saw he could not attain his own false ideal of knowledge, he blamed this on his finite character. Man confused finitude with sin. Thus he commingled the metaphysical and the ethical aspects of reality. Not willing to take the blame for sin, man laid it to circumstances round about him or within him ... Man can never in any sense outgrow his creaturehood. This puts a definite connotation into the expression that man is like God. He is like God, to be sure, but always on a creaturely scale. He can never be like God in God's aseity, immutability, infinity, and unity... Man was not created with comprehensive knowledge. Man was finite and his finitude was originally no burden to him.[xvii]

It would do a lot of us a lot of good to get past any stigma we may have attached to the idea of repenting. Repenting does mean failure, yes. But repenting is not a shameful thing. We will all need to repent and get back on track spiritually over and over again. We should expect this and be happy to repent and come back to the Lord's path. Paul describes godly sorrow as "repentance without regret."[xviii] This would be a much better alternative to guilt. Proverbs 24:16a says that the righteous man may fall seven times, but he gets back up.

I don't want to gloss over the fact that we sin and we are guilty.

Most people in the world believe that mere time rids us of sin. If we wait long enough, then whatever sin we've committed ceases to be a problem. However, time cannot truly heal or forgive sin; only God can do that. And the answer for guilt is not ignoring it; the answer for guilt is the Cross. There may be some mourning involved as we come into the freedom Christ purchased for us. Sometimes, when we have a big secret sin, or habit, or past, it may take a while to see God loosen those chains, but it can be done. I've seen people with incredibly painful lives experience deeper and deeper levels of God's grace and freedom as they take things to Him in prayer and turn to Christian friends and counselors for support.

People can get involved in certain sinful habits that predispose them to more guilt. Pornography is one common example of a habit that creates a cycle of guilt and defeat. Really any addiction works this way. Addictions are different than other sinful areas; and I believe that people with addictions benefit a lot from a regular accountability partner of the same sex who with whom they can be completely honest in a regular relationship.

We may be confused with the idea of dealing with mistakes in the past. When is it ok to put the past behind us? Do we need to make amends or confess our mistakes before we let the guilt go? I hesitate to give an easy answer here. I think that in most cases we would do well to talk about these issues with someone we respect. Then an objective outside voice can speak to our situation. And the two Christians can take the issue to God together. However, when it comes down to it, God knew about our past when He accepted us, and we can rest assured that we are forgiven by Him for any mistakes we have made.

CONCLUSION

When we are mired in guilt feelings, we will doubt the truthfulness of God's diagnosis and slowly sink into unmotivated estrangement. Rather than being assured of what God says, we will experience the opposite. Insecurity is so immobilizing! That is probably why God's enemy loves to attack us in this way. We need to be more objective about our guilt. Either we are guilty, or we are innocent. Even if we are guilty in certain areas, God wants us to approach him boldly and respond with repentance. We do not need to imprison ourselves in bad feelings as punishment for our crimes. God is our Judge; we can leave the sentencing up to Him.

4

SPIRITUAL CONFIDENCE
AND THE WORD

Many Christians lack confidence when it comes to the Bible. I've heard a number of people express frustration and even fatalism in conjunction with their time in the Word. We hear ourselves and others uttering statements such as, "I'm just not much of a reader," "I have trouble paying attention," "I'm just too busy for that," "I don't really understand a lot of it," or even "I am better in other areas like prayer and singing, and I experience a relationship with God that way." There are serious problems with these resigned statements. For one thing, the Bible is an important part of Christian growth and should not be ignored. For another, God has given us a mind and Spirit to know Him and understand His Word.

"For who knows a person's thoughts except the spirit of that person, which is in him? So also no one comprehends the thoughts of God except the Spirit of God. Now we have received not the spirit of the world, but the Spirit who is from God, that we might understand the things freely given us by God" (1 Corinthians 2:11-12 ESV).

BIBLICAL CONFIDENCE

The Bible is vital to our spiritual confidence. Without the Bible we wouldn't have any concrete promises to anchor our thoughts and keep them in the right place. Imagine what it would be like if we had to determine which of our thoughts to trust without a bigger and better standard of measurement on which to rely. Life would be so confusing! People disagree enough already, even with the Bible to look to for guidance.

The Bible is much more than an interesting read. It's one thing to read the Bible and appreciate it mildly; it's another thing to really believe in the ideas and thoughts for life contained within. *Someone confident in the Bible is ready to be instructed by it.* Miles Stanford says, "How often we simply admire and talk about truths the Holy Spirit reveals to us in the Word, whereas His primary purpose in giving them to us is that we might stand upon them in faith, waiting confidently for Him to make them an integral part of our life."[xix]

ATTITUDE ABOUT ALL OF IT

God's Word is eternal and important.[xx] Yet sometimes, when I'm struggling through an especially dry part of Leviticus, I wonder if all parts of God's Word are created equal. However, wondering why certain parts of the Bible were included can cause us to dig deeper and understand things that may not be obvious at first. If we believe that God is the Mastermind behind Scripture, we will have a curious attitude about the entire thing. If we are only interested in certain sections, this may point to a lack of spiritual confidence or a dubious opinion of the canonicity of Scripture. It is helpful to do a study on inspiration and canonicity.[xxi]

G. K. Chesterton said, "What we suffer from today is humility in the wrong place. Modesty has moved from the organ of ambition and settled upon the organ of conviction, where it was never meant to be. A man was meant to be doubtful about himself, but undoubting about the truth; this has been exactly reversed... We are on the road to producing a race of men too mentally modest to believe in the multiplication table."[xxii] In other words, it's not prideful to be confident about truth.

THE WORD IS OUR WEAPON

In the description of our spiritual armor in Ephesians 6, the only weapon mentioned is the sword of the Word.[xxiii] Everything else is defensive armor, but *the Word can do some damage*. 2 Corinthians 10:3-5 says, "For though we walk in the flesh, we are not waging war according to the flesh. For the weapons of our warfare are not of the flesh but have divine power to destroy strongholds. We destroy arguments and every lofty opinion raised against the knowledge of God, and take every thought captive to obey Christ (ESV)." A spiritually confident Christian uses truth from the Word to destroy other thoughts in the battleground of ideas.

When we are experiencing guilty or fearful thoughts, the Bible's truth will remind us who we are and what God has done. When we are feeling self-righteous, the Bible can humble us and remind us of our position. When we are cold, the Bible can begin a fire in our souls for others who need the love of God. Reading the Bible is an activity that endangers our false ideas.

When I'm reading the Bible or listening to someone give a Bible lecture, I'm often flooded with all sorts of fresh ideas and conviction. I can see why the book of Hebrews says: "For the word of God is living and active. Sharper than any double-edged sword, it penetrates even to dividing soul and spirit, joints and marrow; it judges the thoughts and attitudes of the heart" (Hebrews 4:12 NIV). If we, as Christians, subject ourselves to God's truth, then we have nowhere to hide when we are wrong in our thinking. It's a relief to know that we can be corrected in this way, rather than moving forward blindly.

The Bible is also essential when we hope to help our Christian friends. When a friend of ours is under deception, we can use Bible verses to help them see the truth. For example, maybe a friend has been so wrapped up in work that they've failed to come to fellowship meetings for quite some time. You've talked with them about it, but they are convinced that their hands are tied. You can then use Scripture to make a plea that meeting together as Christians is vital to our spiritual health and worth making sacrifices to maintain. It's easy for a friend to find a way to write you off (or any other sinful person); but people have a harder time rejecting God's Word.

Even when we are talking to non-Christians, a well-timed Bible verse that is given in a loving way can plant a seed of truth that God grows in their hearts. And honestly, it will probably do them some good even if it isn't given at the right time or in the right way.

Once, I was sitting at a restaurant studying, and the woman in the booth behind me was sobbing. She was in her mid to late fifties, and she was talking loudly to a friend about how her mother had just passed away. The friend left, but the woman stayed at the table crying. I wanted to say something, but it's not easy for me to just plop down and talk to an crying stranger. So, I just wrote a verse down on a small piece of paper with our church web address on the back. The verse said, "The Lord is near to the broken hearted" (Psalm 34:18a NASB). I just paused awkwardly at the table until she looked up at me and then explained that I couldn't help overhearing, and wanted to give her this verse. Then I quickly took my seat again.

She read the verse and came over to my table and thanked me, sat down and proceeded to talk for a good while about God and the Bible. I saw that day that people can be really touched by a well-timed verse. She was super grateful for my awkward invasion, and it turned into an opportunity for the gospel.

USING SCRIPTURE IN OUR SERVICE OF OTHERS

Whether helping a friend through a difficult time, trying to encourage someone, teaching someone about God, or even praying aloud with others, quoting the Bible will add depth and reality to our own words. God promises that His Word will do something supernatural when people hear it. Consider the following passages:

"For as the rain and snow come down from heaven, and do not return there until they have watered the earth, making it bring forth and sprout, giving seed to the sower and bread to the eater, so shall My Word be that goes out from My mouth; it shall not return to Me empty, but it shall accomplish that which I purpose, and succeed in the thing for which I sent it" (Isaiah 55:10-11 NRSV).

"For the Word of God is living and active, sharper than any two-edged sword, piercing to the division of soul and of spirit, of joints and of marrow, and discerning the thoughts and intentions of the heart" (Hebrews 4:12 NRSV).

"And we also thank God constantly for this, that when you received the Word of God which you heard from us, you accepted it not as the word of men but as what it really is, the Word of God, which is at work in you believers" (1 Thessalonians 2:13 NRSV).

We know from these passages and others like it that God's Word has an effect on those who hear it. It is God's promise. Our own words, however, have no such guarantee. We can't depend on wisdom and wit alone if we want to truly help others grow spiritually. We must become ministers who accurately handle and utilize the Bible.

Second Timothy 3:16-17 says that the Word fully equips us for every good work. Whatever we are doing, whoever we are trying to help, God's Word is useful. It is important to cultivate that voice within us that will call to mind certain pertinent scriptures. Knowing how to use Bible verses is a funny thing – the more we are reading, the more things from other places in the Bible will come to mind. However, if we're away from it for a while, we will begin to forget even the things we used to know well.

OUR RELATIONSHIP TO THE WORD SUMMED UP

"Sir Arthur Blackwell says a Christian's relationship to the Word can be summed up in four words:

- **Admit** – Open your whole being to let it be flooded with light. Let the truth in. Study the Bible sympathetically and lovingly. Let it be God's voice to you direct.
- **Submit** – Let the truth grip you and govern you. Let the plain declarations of God's Word be the end of all controversy.
- **Commit** – Let today's message be articulated to yesterday's so that a chain is forged that is a veritable anchor to your soul in times of trouble and trail. Grip the truth by hiding it in your heart
- **Transmit** – Don't be a pool; be a stream. Don't hoard your riches; Share the bounties of the Lord's table with another. Make every truth tenfold your own by passing it on."[xxiv]

5

SPIRITUAL CONFIDENCE
AND PRAYER

At times, I've found myself praying for something so passionately that I suddenly realize my attitude about God is pretty poor. In a way, I sometimes pray as though I believed that I care more about people than God does. It's not that passion is a bad thing by any means, but sometimes I can forget to listen. I can petition God for things like crazy, especially when I'm scared, but I can easily fail to spend serious time trying to communicate. How bizarre it would be if I talked to my husband or friend the way I sometimes "talk" to God. It's not really communicating at all – it's more like quickly barking out a list of desires, or letting out a whine and then promptly leaving the room. This is the vision of a truly immature prayer life. Yet I know that a better, more spiritually confident, prayer life is possible.

We should feel free to tell God anything in prayer, but we also need to be willing to receive correction from Him as we pray. God can change our whole attitude and outlook during a time of prayer. He shows us something better than the thoughts we concoct from ourselves. He often calls people to mind as we pray, and gives us ideas for how to love them. He instructs us about Himself, and about ourselves. He also can comfort us, causing us to feel a sense of peace. And He trumps the wisdom of the world system and of Satan when we are being deceived.

If, at times, we notice how weak and limited we truly are – we will begin to see the deep and powerful need for prayer. As J. Oswald Sanders puts it, "In one moment prayer can lay hold of God and bind the devil. It can be focused on a single objective and it can roam the world. It invests puny man with a sort of limitless power, for 'all things are possible to him that believeth' " -Mark 9:23b KJV."xxv Our need for prayer becomes abundantly clear to us when we are in a difficult situation and feel completely helpless. How awesome it would be to realize that need in all situations!

BOLD ACCESS

Imagine what it would be like to live next door to C.S. Lewis, George MacDonald, or any other respected Christian thinker. What if they lived next to me, and they told me that they were always home and that I could come over and talk whenever I liked. I would make them sorry they said that! I would go over there with questions and ask for advice in different areas. If I didn't have anything to talk about, I would happily go over and just listen to whatever they wanted to tell me. This is the kind of situation many Christians long for, yet our unlimited access to God is much better than access to a great Christian thinker. It's almost insane to think of how we fail to take advantage of this awesome opportunity.

People can let us down, or let us go, but God will not. As Christians, we are privileged to have an everlasting, trustworthy, and intimate relationship with Him. A relationship we have access to, through prayer, no matter where we are or what is happening. More than that, God has more to offer as an ally than any person ever could.

Psalm 16:8 states, I have set the LORD always before me; because He is at my right hand, I shall not be shaken.

If I were thrown into a jail cell for the rest of my life, I could still communicate with Someone. I always have with me the Bread of Life who can give my soul a feast.

ASKING AND ANSWERS

James 4:2b says, "You do not have because you do not ask." Jesus brought up a similar concept when he said, "Ask and it will be given to you; seek and you will find, knock and the door will be opened to you" (Matthew 7:7 NAB). We need to ask God for things. We need to ask in faith, and believe He will do amazing things when the time is right. God *does* answer our prayers! That isn't just a platitude or a thing mystical people say – it is a biblical truth in which we can have confidence.

When we lack spiritual confidence we fail to ask God for things. Rather, it may be a temptation to think of ways to get things for ourselves. Even while praying, we may be thinking about asking God to help us with a difficult friendship, but then instead of asking Him about it, we begin thinking of things we could say to get their attention in some way or another. It's possible to view asking for God's help as a last resort. This may happen as a result of self-confidence or lack of faith in the effectiveness of prayer. Prayer almost becomes like wishing; it is only done when we are out of options.

John talks about answered prayer in 1 John 5:14-15; "This is the confidence which we have before Him, that, if we ask anything according to His will, He hears us. And if we know that He hears us in whatever we ask, we know that we have the requests which we have asked from Him" (NASB).

APPROPRIATION AND GRATITUDE

J. Stuart Holden describes a mature prayer life this way:
If we have any desire for His power, our desire is not original but merely responsive to His desire, and hence we make a profound mistake in constantly praying for what God has already given, and in continuing to ask when God would have us take. Such prayer is not the voice of faith, however earnest

it may be, but rather it is the expression of unsuspected unbelief ... [God] must be trusted to make good His word. Reckoning that the promise is fulfilled, the soul must now step out to do the next obvious duty and face the next difficulty in the life of service, expecting that the Spirit's power will be manifested.[xxvi] -J. Holden

Put simply, this means that we should keep the promises of God in mind as we pray. It may be necessary to correct ourselves while praying. For example, we may start out saying, "I wish that you would forgive me" but then change it to, "I'm grateful that You have forgiven me, I pray that You would help me realize that forgiveness more." If we are to have a prayer life like the one J. Stuart Holden describes, we need to be studying the Word. As Evan Hopkins says, "Faith needs facts to rest upon. Presumption can take fancy instead of fact. God, in His Word, reveals to us the facts with which faith has to deal."[xxvii]

In *The Green Letters*, Miles Stanford puts it this way: "The two realities of seeing and needing bring us from childish meandering into a responsible, specific walk of faith. They take us from the 'help me' attitude to that of giving thanks; from begging to appropriation."[xxviii]

If we are remembering God's promises and truth while we pray, it will make us more grateful. Rather than the bleak portrait I painted of myself at the start of this chapter, we will come to God thanking Him for all He is doing. In addition, we will be more interested in finding out what He is up to and how we can be a part of it. John depicted this as "abiding in the Vine" in John 15. This word picture of a vine and branches shows us how relational and dependant we can be in prayer. The imagery is striking – where would a branch be if it wasn't attached to its vine?

WARFARE

Prayer has been described as the rest of faith, and the fight of faith.[xxix] Prayer is not just warm and fuzzy. *Prayer can be a battle*. In an article I love, prayer is called an act of rebellion.[xxx] When we pray, we rebel against the status quo – against the wisdom of the world and against the lies of Satan. Prayer can be fiercely powerful.

Samuel Chadwick said this of Satan: "He laughs at our toil, mocks our wisdom, but trembles when we pray."[xxxi]

PERSISTENCE

"He told them a parable *to the effect that they ought always to pray and not lose heart*. He said, 'In a certain city there was a judge who neither feared God nor respected man. And there was a widow in that city who kept coming to him saying, 'Give me justice against my adversary.' For a while he refused, but afterward he said to himself, 'Though I neither fear God nor respect man, yet because this widow keeps bothering me, I will give her justice, so that she will not beat me down with her continual coming.' And the Lord said, 'Hear what the unrighteous judge says. And will not God give justice to His elect, who cry to Him day and night? Will He delay long over them? I tell you, He will give justice to them speedily. Nevertheless, *when the Son of Man comes, will He find faith on earth?*'" (Luke 18:1-8 ESV, emphasis added).

I used to be kind of confused by the idea of persistent prayer. Why does God want us to repeat ourselves over and over again? However, that all changed when my little brother Joe got into a bad accident. He was riding his bicycle and was hit by a car. He had a chest tube, seven broken ribs, a collapsed lung, a bleeding spleen and liver, and a head injury that included bleeding in his brain. Needless to say, this was all I was thinking about. I was praying for Joe over and over – maybe fifty times a day or more. But it wasn't just that; I talked about how Joe was doing with every friend I talked to. And suddenly, persistent prayer made a lot of sense. I'm talking about what is on my mind. How bizarre would it be to see a friend and not mention Joe? Or imagine if a husband told a wife, "I've decided I don't need to tell you that I love you anymore. I've already said that once before, what's the point in repeating it?" Both things would be ludicrous, because part of relational closeness involves repeating ourselves, especially if the topic is one that causes us to be passionate or troubled. Offering God anything less would be to place Him in an impersonal catergory.

But what about the idea of "meaningless repetition" brought up in Matthew 6:7? Jesus says, "They think they will be heard by their many words;" Is that what we are doing when we are persisting in prayer the way the widow persisted with the wicked judge? The answer is no. Persisting isn't meant to be magical. We aren't making God do what we want by using a confusing incantation on Him. No, we are persisting in prayer and *not losing heart*, as it says in the beginning of that passage. Persisting in prayer is about keeping our faith in a difficult situation. And just like the wicked judge eventually answered the widow's request, God may answer us too – if it is within His will.

Thankfully, my brother eventually got better. And whether he got better or not, I was grateful that persistent prayer had helped me to not lose heart.

Praying in the Spirit

God has promised to help us as we pray. This means that we can be guided in prayer, almost moldable. Rather than only saying things, we can try to be more receptive and responsive. For example, if you're praying and an unexpected friend comes to mind, you could keep in mind that God may be bringing that person up to you for a reason. We could even take it as a cue to move toward that person in love, hoping that while we relate and talk, more will come to light. This is spiritual confidence, belief that something spiritual and real is occurring when we pray. And believing that prayer is relational, not just one-sided.

ACTION

The best prayer life will be the prayer life of the person who is out on the streets getting in there with messy people and their messy lives. Being an active Christian completely changes what our prayer life looks like. We subtly know which things really matter and which things are just fluff. It's when we're far away from the needs of others that our walk in prayer is like a man meandering through the mist.

Therefore, the best step we can take to improve our prayer life, is the step outside. We need to go and find someone else that needs our help. Period. If we feel like we're looking everywhere and can't find anyone, we are fooling ourselves. There are people in every city who need love, friendship, food, and most of all God. We just need to prioritize looking for them.

"Why faint when you may be strong? Why suffer defeat when you may conquer? Take your wavering faith and drooping spirit to Him who can revive and replenish them." –C.H. Spurgeon

SPIRITUAL CONFIDENCE
AND SUFFERING

When Christians offer simple platitudes to suffering people, they call wrath upon themselves. Rightly so, as suffering is not something for which there is an easy answer. But, we can't let fear of being "that guy" keep us from encouraging suffering people. We need to look deeply at a theology of suffering, try to understand it for ourselves and others, and then, if we can, learn the Biblical secret of rejoicing in the midst of suffering.

When we suffer, it's easy to wonder "who is at fault?" I believe this comes from a poor theology of suffering - whether we blame ourselves, others or God. It's popular even in secular circles to hear the platitude, "everything happens for a reason." Maybe it does, but I'm not sure that we can be confident of that. What about the tower of Siloam? In Luke 13:1-5, Jesus explains:

> There were some present at that very time who told Him about the Galileans whose blood Pilate had mingled with their sacrifices. And he answered them, 'Do you think that these Galileans were worse sinners than all the other Galileans, because they suffered in this way? No, I tell you; but unless you repent, you will all likewise perish. Or those eighteen on whom the tower in Siloam fell and killed them: do you think

that they were worse offenders than all the others who
lived in Jerusalem? No, I tell you; but unless you
repent, you will all likewise perish" (NRSV).

Jesus brings up two tragedies: Pilate murdering some
Galileans, and a tower falling and killing 18 people. For both of these
tragedies he gives assurance that these people didn't suffer as
punishment for extensive sinning. Basically, they were in the wrong
place at the wrong time. In the first tragedy we see how people like
Pilate can use their free will to cause suffering. In the second tragedy,
we can see that bad things sometimes happen as a result of this fallen
world. Buildings fall. It doesn't necessarily mean anything. People
choose to kill and torture others. This isn't necessarily a statement
about what God thinks.

A FALLEN WORLD

"For I consider that the sufferings of this present time
are not worth comparing with the glory that is to be
revealed to us. For the creation waits with eager
longing for the revealing of the sons of God. For the
creation was subjected to futility, not willingly, but
because of him who subjected it, in hope that the
creation itself will be set free its bondage to corruption
and obtain the freedom of the glory of the children
of God. For we know that the whole creation has been
groaning together in the pains of childbirth until now.
And not only the creation, but we ourselves, who have
the firstfruits of the Spirit, groan inwardly as we wait
eagerly for adoption as sons, the redemption of our
bodies" (Romans 8:18-23 ESV).

Both the creation and our own broken bodies groan to be
finished with this time of fallenness and suffering. Disease, death,
natural disasters, lack of resources, and more, happen as a result of

the choice Adam and Eve made to reject God's leadership and the subsequent degeneration of the earth. Furthermore, things like murder, rape, child abuse and neglect, greed, and the like can be attributed to human free will.

When I was in college, a group of Christian demonstrators came to campus wearing t-shirts that said HIV was God's punishment for homosexuality. It really embarrassed me, and I've often thought about that group and the theology they were displaying to my non-Christian friends. I wonder what they were hoping to accomplish, and I wonder how they could seem so sure that God had intervened in that specific way. And I wondered what they think about all of the innocent babies who contract that virus. I think these kinds of emphatic statements about suffering should be avoided. It's presumptuous, not to mention ugly. If we are speculating, we should present it that way rather than having what I'll call "subjective confidence." Making presumptions about God and then confidently assuring people that those presumptions are trustworthy reminds me of the Old Testament crime of false prophecy. False prophets spoke their own ideas as though they came from the Lord.

PUNITIVE SUFFERING AND PERSECUTION

"Beloved, do not be surprised at the fiery trial when it comes upon you to test you, as though something strange were happening to you. But rejoice insofar as you share in Christ's sufferings, that you may also rejoice and be glad when His glory is revealed. If you are insulted for the name of Christ, you are blessed, because the Spirit of glory and God rests on you. But let none of you suffer as a murderer or a thief or an evildoer or as a meddler. Yet if anyone suffers as a Christian, let him not be ashamed, but let him glorify God in that name" (1 Peter 4:12-16 ESV).

It's possible to suffer as a result of our own free will choices. Sometimes we suffer as a result of bad choices, for instance we could choose to steal a car and then suffer in jail. This is punitive suffering. Or we could, as Christians, suffer for our good choices. A secular mother may refuse to let her Christian daughter attend church. This is persecution. When we suffer for our beliefs, Peter urges us not to be ashamed. Persecution is rough, but we are in the company of Christ when we suffer in this way.

GOD'S DISCIPLINE

God's discipline is a different kind of suffering. As we mature as Christians, pieces of our old sinful nature die. Sometimes it can be a painful death. We say goodbye to sins we used to really rely on and take identity from. However, this sort of suffering is a really positive thing. Just as my kids complain about being in school all day, yet it is for their own good to learn basic knowledge; so our growing pains are for our own good.

In his book, "Release of the Spirit," Watchman Nee refers to this particular kind of suffering as "the breaking of the outer man." The Bible often uses the imagery of a smelters fire refining a metal. The end result is wholesomeness. While breaking may be painful, it would be much more painful to be left alone to our own devices. Imagine a child who always got what he wanted. What an unpleasant and unhappy adult he would turn out to be!

"For at the moment all discipline seems painful rather than pleasant, but later it yields the peaceful fruit of righteousness to those who have been trained by it" (Hebrews 12:11 ESV).

WHAT WE CAN BE CONFIDENT ABOUT

"You ought to begin your day with this confidence, that you have enough in Christ to meet every difficulty that may befall you." –J.B. Stoney

When faced with extreme suffering, we suddenly realize how much we need God. God is the only One with the power to help us in certain situations. We grow extremely grateful that at least we have Him in which to turn. Not only this, but God is able to sympathize with our suffering, since He Himself suffered so much while on earth. "Let us then with confidence draw near to the throne of grace, that we may receive mercy and find grace to help in time of need" (Hebrews 4:16ESV).

God is our Advocate; our Defense and our Light. "The LORD is my light and my salvation: whom shall I fear? The Lord is the stronghold of my life; of whom shall I be afraid? Though an army encamp against me, my heart will not fear; though war arise against me, yet I will be confident" (Psalm 27:1, 3 ESV). God offers us comfort, strength, perseverance, encouragement, joy, and peace.[xxxii] These are the sorts of things we can be confident of during times of suffering. Daniel chapter three recounts the story of King Nebuchadnezzar throwing people into a furnace because they wouldn't bow down to a golden statue of him. When he asks them if they have any final words, they say that their God is able to save them and that even if He doesn't they still won't worship the statue. This is the sort of stance we should strive to emulate. The stance that we know God can put an end to our suffering, and we are loyal to Him even if He chooses not to end it. The Bible calls people of this caliber, "men of whom the world is not worthy" (Hebrews 11:38a).

Another important truth that we should be confident of, is that God will make all things right someday. Not only will He deal with injustice, He will put an end to suffering.

> "I believe like a child that suffering will be healed and made up for, that all the humiliating absurdity of human contradictions will vanish like a pitiful mirage, like the despicable fabrication of the impotent and infinitely small mind of man, that in the world's finale, at the moment of eternal harmony, something so precious will come to pass that it will suffice for all

hearts, for the comforting of resentments, for the atonement of all crimes of humanity, of all the blood they've shed; that it will make it not only possible to forgive but to justify all that has happened." –Fyodor Dostoevsky[xxxiii]

WHAT SHOULD WE DO?

It's important in times of suffering to be wary of our favorite sins. Suffering can bring out the best in us, but also the worst in us. Job 36:21 warns, "Be careful that you do not choose evil because you have preferred it to suffering."

We can't turn against God at times like these. It's like having a broken arm and raging against the doctor who is trying to set it. "Therefore let those who suffer according to God's will entrust their souls to a faithful Creator while doing good" (1 Peter 4:19 ESV).

Before David was king, he lived for a time in the city of Ziklag. One day, he and his army of 600 men went out and left all their possessions, their wives, and their children at home in the city. On the day they came back to the city, they had walked for 50 miles. Coming into the city, they found their homes burned to the ground and their families kidnapped. After sobbing until "they had no more strength to weep," they considered killing David because they were "bitter in soul for their families." I can understand being that upset, but David didn't deserve people turning on him. David's family was kidnapped too, and his home burned.

David shows in this chapter (1 Samuel 30) how to react well when suffering. It says that he "strengthened himself in the Lord" and "inquired of the Lord." David never turned against God. Not before the trial, not during it, and not after. After this story ends in victory and celebration, with the reuniting of all the families, David is still giving credit to God and showing loyalty to Him. He doesn't say to God, "Alright, thanks … I can take it from here."

"I love those who can smile in trouble, who can gather strength from distress, and grow brave by reflection. 'Tis the business of little minds to shrink, but they whose heart is firm, and whose conscience approves their conduct, will pursue their principles unto death." -Leonardo da Vinci

7

FEAR

Spiritual confidence has been defined here as assured spiritual belief resulting in bold spiritual action. While guilt erodes our assured spiritual belief and closeness with God, fear erodes our bold spiritual action with others.

WHAT'S WRONG WITH FEAR?

"Whoever confesses that Jesus is the Son of God, God abides in him, and he in God. So we have come to know and to believe the love God has for us ... By this is love perfected with us, so that we may have confidence for the day of judgment, because as he is so also are we in this world. There is no fear in love, but perfect love casts out fear. For fear has to do with punishment, and whoever fears has not been perfected in love" (1 John 4:15-18 ESV).

"For you did not receive the spirit of slavery to fall back to fear, but you have received the Spirit of adoption as sons, by whom we cry, 'Abba! Father!'" (Romans 8:15 ESV).

In these passages, there is a picture of God's love chasing away our fear; literally casting out fear by the new Spirit of love He has given us. And when this loves matures, or is perfected, we are left with confidence.

There are a few clues in these two passages about what is wrong with fear. For one thing, fear is connected with slavery. When we are fearful, we are caught in an addicting trap. Soon, we are no longer the ones making the calls – we are slaves obeying the commands of fear. I've been in situations where I've felt so shy and unsure of myself, I almost felt physically unable to speak. Fear can seem like something in our bodies, making us freeze. Wouldn't it be nice to be freed from the different hang-ups and insecurities that keep us motionless?

Another problem with fear mentioned above, is that fear has to do with punishment and God has made it abundantly clear that we are no longer in danger of punishment from Him. So, we see that fear is also tied to unbelief. Many fears come down to the general insecurity that we don't want to be unlovely, alone, or insignificant. If we really understood God's attitude and stance toward us, we would know that we already possess significance, secure relationship, and love.

Furthermore, we should know that our insecurities and posturing don't bring us any closer to anyone. People are drawn to sincerity. And our fears about others often turn out to have a "self-fulfilling prophecy" effect. I can't speak for others about this, but I can say that, personally, I love to have friends who aren't afraid of me or afraid of what I think. Those brave few are my closest friends.

I've heard it said that "fear not" is the most frequent command in the Bible. I haven't done the research to know for sure if that's true or not, but it makes a certain amount of sense when we consider both the Old and New Testaments. Whether that statistic is right or not though, it seems clear that God really doesn't want us to be stuck in a fearful lifestyle. It's not that He is an uncaring drill sergeant telling us to quit being wimps, He wants something better for us.

IS FEAR EVER GOOD?

The Bible does seem to indicate that there is a time and a place for appropriate fear. So, when is fear healthy and when is it unhealthy?

Usually the unhealthy fear that is spoken of in the Bible is what we might call a "shrinking fear." Unhealthy fear makes us shrink back from taking action. Likewise, healthy fear could be understood as a "healthy respect." As children we learn a healthy respect for the hot stove, and as Christians there are certain areas where healthy respect is still very appropriate.

God Himself is a Being worthy of healthy respect. And if "fear not" is a popular phrase in the Bible, "fear God" certainly rivals it. "The fear of the Lord is the beginning of knowledge; but fools despise wisdom and instruction" (Proverbs 1:7). In Hebrews 12, the author brings up how scared the people were when Moses received the Ten Commandments – and instead of spurning their attitude, tells us that we should feel the same way. There are some serious phrases in that passage, such as, "See that you do not refuse him who is speaking ... let us be grateful for receiving a kingdom that cannot be shaken, and thus let us offer to God acceptable worship, with reverence and awe, for our God is a consuming fire."[xxxiv] We don't need to fear God's punishment as the verse at the start of this chapter says, but we do need to take God seriously. Healthy respect for something means we aren't treating it flippantly.

We also need to cultivate a healthy respect for the evil we are capable of perpetrating. Some circles of Christians refer to this attitude as "fear of the flesh." In first Corinthians ten, we are warned to think about the example of the Israelites during their wanderings in the desert, it ends that description with this saying, "Now these things happened to them as an example, but they were written down for our instruction, on whom the end of the ages has come. Therefore let anyone who thinks that he stands firm, take heed lest he fall" (1 Corinthians 10:11-12 ESV). Also, in Hebrews we are given a similar warning: "Therefore, while the promise of entering His rest stands, let us fear lest any of you should seem to have failed to reach it" (Hebrews 4:1 ESV). We may think that our lives are going well, but we need to know that we are all capable of great betrayals and failures.

Shrinking fear, on the other hand, has more to do with staying out of the fray. Whether we like to avoid conflict, avoid consequences, avoid others, avoid suffering, or avoid adventure; shrinking fear means that we keep ourselves safe and comfortable. This sort of fear comes in all shapes and sizes. And believe me when I say (from personal experience) that those with the biggest bark have some of the biggest fears. No one is immune from this unhealthy, crippling, broken and unloved emotion.

FIGHTING FEAR

A few years ago I did a study on the verses about fear in the wisdom literature. I noticed that a lot of times when fear was mentioned, the ideas of "God is with me" and "God is for me" were mentioned alongside.[xxxv] That really stuck with me. Subsequently, when I've felt fearful, I pray and thank God for those two truths. And I must say, it is very comforting to remember that God is with me and for me. Those truths speak to the very heart of our fears, and overpower our fearful thoughts. *Love triumphs over fear just as mercy triumphs over judgment.*

One of the best ways to gain courage is to try new things. We need to move things out of the "unknown" category of fear. If we can conjure up the courage to try something new, we often find that thing losing its mystique and the fear of it fades. We may be afraid to tell the gospel to a particularly scary person, but once we have – even if they call us stupid and reject the idea entirely – we find that it wasn't so hard after all.

People with a good deal of humility are often more brave than grandstanding folks who are all bark and no bite. When we aren't worried about our own standing, we will be willing to try new things even if we fail. Rather than being worried about the status quo, we can let humility take us into uncharted waters. And I think God is often into developing humility and bravery alongside each other.

Finally, it is helpful for us to recognize when we've done all we can in a particular area. It is brave to try and make things better when there is something to do. However, in many cases when we're scared, there isn't anything at all we can do about it. We should be willing to let some of our anxious thoughts go. When we take the Lord into our confidence and tell him our feelings during these times, we may find the Spirit within drumming up all kinds of unexpected courage.

UNSAFE LIVES

If we want spiritually confident lives, we may need to stop worrying so much about our own safety. "Well, it is but a little while and He will appear to answer all questions and to wipe away all tears. I would not wish, then, to be one of those who had none to wipe away. Would you?"[xxxv] There are worse things than heartbreak – there is uselessness. In the book *The Four Loves* by C.S. Lewis he has a pretty dramatic passage about fear-inspired self-protection:

"There is no safe investment. To love at all is to be vulnerable. Love anything, and your heart will certainly be wrung and possibly broken. If you want to make sure of keeping it intact, you must give your heart to no one, not even to an animal. Wrap it carefully round with hobbies and little luxuries; avoid all entanglements; lock it up safe in the casket or coffin of your selfishness. But in that casket – safe, dark, motionless, airless – it will change. It will not be broken; it will become unbreakable."[xxxvii]

Yikes! There is nothing that inspires more bravery in me than thoughts like these. I would rather try and be terrible at something than go my whole life playing it safe.

Many Christians are willing to stay on the sidelines and let more "dynamic personalities" do all the speaking for God. I've noticed that there are many people who not only know that they are timid when it comes to doing the Lord's work, but they accept that about themselves! No. We cannot be content with this. God has commissioned all of us with the ministry of reconciliation[xxxviii], and we must at least make an effort to help others spiritually.

> "There is no reserve in God's love; He has given the best in heaven for the worst on earth, and in this way He has rebuked distrust and established confidence." –Miles Stanford

SPIRITUAL CONFIDENCE WITH OTHERS

When we talk about having spiritual confidence with others, we'll talk first about fellowship and friendship with others, and then we'll talk about specific areas of Christian ministry.

FELLOWSHIP

God promises that His church will be victorious in the end. Even though our fellowships may be floundering, we are "more than conquerors in Him."[xxxix] Knowing where we will end up can raise our spirits when things look bleak. It can also give us an appreciation for the members of the universal church. We're all part of the same team; and it will be the winning team in the end.

God supplies Christians with unity and love. Even if we're not gifted relationally, God has changed that by giving us a "Spirit of love and power."[xl] Christians who fail to relate to other Christians are denying an important part of their new natures. Also, it is against God's plan for us to be isolated and disunited from the Body of Christ.

Having close Christian friends should become an important priority for us. Also, meeting together with a group of Christians should be a priority. And it's not enough really to meet together with other Christians and just chat about life; we need to be opening the Bible together and praying together. If we are confident that this is a worthwhile use of our time, we will see this beginning to happen even in unexpected ways. Maybe our church has pretty shallow relationships, but we can still have deep fellowship by inviting a few Christians over to do a Bible study at our homes. I've had many Bible studies meet in my home, and it is a fantastic thing. Real spiritual needs are exposed and met. Non-Christian friends come and decide to begin relationships with God. Christians become really excited about God and what He's doing. There is nothing better. And for those of us who are parents, it makes an important statement to our children. I was raised in a home filled with visitors and open Bibles and prayer, and it left a lasting impression on me that people are worth our time, and God is a part of everyday life. I'm honored to have my children growing up in a similar home.

I've made a few mistakes in the area of starting new Bible study groups. For one thing, I've found that it is a mistake to act embarrassed about wanting to read the Bible and pray. If I am mumbling and shrugging my shoulders and making a half-hearted suggestion, people will respond with half-hearted shoulder shrugs. But if I am excited to do it, people often get on board and feel excited too. Our confidence about the goodness of deep fellowship will go a long way in helping the attitudes of the others around us. When we feel like telemarketers, ashamed that we are interrupting someone's personal time, we will be as ineffective as telemarketers.

EVANGELISM

God is greatly involved in evangelism – maybe more than we realize. He is there before we are, while we are, and after we have gone. If we understand His involvement, we will have much more spiritual confidence in this arena.

God draws all men to Himself, and convicts them of the truth.[xli] Before anyone ever speaks to a non-Christian, God has been speaking to them first. Something inside of each of us has been made aware that God is real, even if we've suppressed that conviction. As an evangelist, it's nice to know that it's not all up to me to introduce someone to God. God has already introduced Himself.

Furthermore, God helps us in the very act of giving the gospel. He can show us opportunities, or "open doors."[xlii] He can bring thoughts and verses to mind as we're speaking.[xliii] And He manifests His "aroma,"[xliv] or perceptible essence, through Believers as they interact with others.

Lastly, after we've left the conversation, God can use the truths and verses we've quoted to continue to bring Himself up within that person's mind. Even if we leave a conversation feeling rejected, we can have faith that God may use the conversation after all.

A few years back, I was in California talking to a youth pastor who appeared to be very successful in evangelism. He said something that really helped me have more spiritual confidence while giving the gospel and building friendships with non-Christians. He said, "What is there to be afraid of? Our King is inviting people into His Kingdom, He's right there with us when we're telling people about it. Even in the darkest home in the darkest corner of the city, we have the upper hand because we have Him with us."

I think it's also a good idea to develop a strong theology of failure.[xlv] Evangelism seems to be one area that can become a big sore spot for many Christians. It shouldn't be that way; this is one of the most joyful things in the Kingdom. But, honestly, I don't know many people who have been immune to discouragement in this area. I think it makes sense on one level; since we are kidnapping from the enemy of God. Satan has a clear motive for keeping us feeling weak in this endeavor. But, whatever the reason, we have to perservere. Without the reaching of non-Christians, our own Christian fellowships become pretty ingrown and unhappy. Our mission as Christians is to be like our Master, who came "to seek and to save that which is lost" (Luke 19:10).

DISCIPLE-MAKING

When Jesus commissioned Believers to make disciples in Matthew 28, He let us know that He is always with us. As we help younger Christians to grow with God, God is there helping the process to move forward in a number of ways. Our job, really, is to train and teach people what we've learned. We are facilitators, or teachers. But each person we mentor is actually a disciple of Christ.

There is an interesting passage about this in first Corinthians three, where Paul talks about the different roles he and Apollos took with some of the Corinthian Believers. In this passage, Paul sheds some light on God's role in the whole process of disciple-making. He writes:

> "What then is Apollos? What is Paul? <u>Servants</u> through whom you believed as the *Lord assigned to each*. I <u>planted</u>. Apollos <u>watered</u>, but *God gave the growth*. So neither the one who plants nor he who waters is anything, but only *God who gives the growth*. He who plants and he who waters are one and each will receive his wages according to his <u>labor</u>. For <u>we are God's fellow workers</u>. You are *God's field, God's building*. According to *the grace of God given to me*, like a skilled master builder <u>I laid a foundation</u>, and someone else is *building upon it*. Let each one <u>take care how he builds</u>" (1 Corinthians 3:5-10, emphasis added).

The italicized portions show God's role, while the underlined portions show our role.

In this Bible version, the ESV, it uses the term "assigned to each." But other versions say that God "gives opportunities" which I like better. God brings people together, and shows us opportunities to help others. He also "gives the growth." We can teach things to people until we are blue in the face, but ultimately we cannot make people grow. People's spiritual growth is a thing between them and God. We just help facilitate spiritual growth. Furthermore, this passage shows that God will reward us in heaven for the spiritual work we did on earth. And it shows that God's people are His people; His "field," His "building." Many Christian workers take too much responsibility for others – we are not responsible *for* others, we are responsible *to* others. The Church belongs to God. Lastly, this passage shows that we are able to minister by the grace God has given us. Ministry isn't really about deserving; it is a grace just as salvation is a grace. The human-centered Christian will need to reflect deeply on truths like these.

"We are God's fellow workers." Human agency is important to disciple-making too. We have a role to play. This passage describes our role as "servants." It further describes the service as 1. "Planting," or later "laying a foundation" and 2. "Watering," or "building on that foundation." So, whether we are helping brand new Christians begin a relationship with God, or whether we are helping established Christians to grow, we have a role in ministering to others. Furthermore, this passage says that we should be careful how we "build" or "labor." We have a real responsibility here. It's not as important as the role God plays with others, but it is important nonetheless. It's important to help others if we can. Becoming a Christian is like getting a new citizenship in a new country that we are very unfamiliar with, and having a guide who already lives there can be a valuable blessing. Those who struggle with super-spirituality should take special note of the human agency being taught in this passage.

For a more in-depth look at disciple-making, refer to the book Dennis McCallum and I co-authored entitled, "Organic Disciple Making." The book delves specifically into mentoring others into spiritual maturity and leadership.

TEACHING

Another aspect of ministry is teaching the Bible to others. Whether we get up in front of a large group and preach, lead a small home Bible study, teach a spiritual class, or just help our friends to remember certain biblical truths; we should be teaching. Teaching is an aspect of disciple-making and evangelism, but teaching also stands alone as a specific kind of service.

I've heard it said that public speaking is most people's number-one fear. It can be very daunting to teach others. We struggle with thoughts about our own inadequacies, and worry how our words will be received. However, it is very possible for even the most reticent among us to develop spiritual confidence in this area.

Not everyone is gifted for teaching to a large group, but every Christian should be able to teach others in some capacity. If someone has been a Christian for one week, they've probably learned a few things that they could teach to someone who has been a Christian for one day.

We've already learned that God's Word has an effect on those who hear it. So, all we really need to do is quote the Bible to someone, and we've facilitated God's work in that person. A few years ago, I was leading a high school home church for a short period of time. One night, the guy who was supposed to teach showed up without a teaching. He hadn't even looked at the passage he was supposed to teach. I told him that he would have to get up and do something anyway, and asked if he would rather use the five minutes we had before the meeting to look over the passage or to pray. He said, "Let's pray." We did, and then he opened up the Bible and gave an amazing teaching that all the kids loved.

When we teach others in the power of the Holy Spirit, God gives us "spiritual thoughts" and "spiritual words." Seen in this light, teaching isn't so scary after all. We are just vehicles for His message.

On the other hand, there are some things that we can do to

become better teachers. We can learn the Bible well, for one thing. If we are constantly learning, we will surprise ourselves with what God can bring to mind in different situations. We will be better prepared to teach if we are in the habit of regular study. One other area of human responsibility is that of presentation. How we present the truth can be a big turn-off to some, but if we work on our presentation, we can silence that critique. We may come off as boring, condescending, or even weird – but if we work on how we present ourselves, we can be less in the way of the message.

LEADING

Some of us are Christian leaders, and even those that aren't usually deal with Christian leaders. So it can be helpful to think about what the Bible has to say concerning leadership. Even if we aren't leaders, our view of leadership will often affect others.

There are many excellent Christian books on this topic,[xlvi] so I'll be brief. God is the true Leader of the church, or "Head" of the body. It is ultimately to Him that we must all answer. However, it is God's will to delegate leadership responsibility to some members of the Church.

It seems from a number of passages in the Bible that it is God who appoints us to service and empowers us to do the task at hand. But it also seems clear that we have steps we need to take in order to become better leaders.

God is the one who brings us to leadership. He gives us the opportunities for service in the same way that He gives us forgiveness – not because we deserve it. Second Corinthians 4:1 says, "Therefore, since we have received this ministry by the mercy of God, we do not lose heart"(ESV). So, the great secret is to keep a strong heart but not take pride from our position. If we could see ministry as an undeserved grace of God, we could enjoy it without becoming egotistical from it.

Francis Bacon says, "He that gives good advice, builds with one hand; he that gives good counsel and example, builds with both; but he that gives good admonition and bad example, builds with one hand and pulls down with the other." It's important that we are watching our lives and our teaching as leaders. Just as Paul recommended to Timothy, we should: "Keep a close watch on yourself and on the teaching" (1 Timothy 4:16a). While leadership is from God and empowered by God, He gives us real responsibility as leaders to lead by example and to teach with truth.

I've sometimes noticed that when I am becoming super-spiritual, I might "coast" as a leader. In other words, I may just re-do teachings I've already done in the past, do a half-hearted three-second prayer about the people in the church, and I may say sanctimonious things about how if people want to move forward with God they can take the steps forward without my help. That's just me ignoring my responsibility. When I actually get proactive about people and church structures and teachings, I see a tangible result. God gets behind that sort of initiative from His leaders. It's not that He is unable to work through us when we are coasting, believe me, I know for a fact He often does just that. It is that the responsibility He gives us is real; we are not just figure-heads.

Hebrews 13:17 suggests that people, "Obey your leaders and submit to them, for they are keeping watch over your souls, as those who will have to give an account"(ESV). If I think about that truth from the perspective of a leader, it means that I should be keeping watch over the souls in the church and that someday I will be testifying about what I learned. When I am coasting, and I read that, I know that it's time to shut off the autopilot.

SERVING

All of us should be excited to serve others. This is one area of ministry that is wide open for creative expression. There are many ways to do helpful things for others. We may help someone move. We may write a kind letter. We may mow someone's lawn or cook them a meal. We may visit people in the hospital or in jail or in a nursing home. We may involve ourselves in community service. We may begin a public garden in a poor neighborhood, work in a food pantry or babysit for a parent who really needs a night to herself.

It's exciting to think of all the ways we could serve, but it can also be overwhelming! If we don't have spiritual confidence in this area, we probably don't know where to start and give up before we even get going. I'm overwhelmed at the thought of all the good things I could be doing with my time. Luckily, God is at work in this ministry too. First Corinthians 16:9 implies that God can open a door for effective service. Also, Romans seven explains: "Likewise, my brothers, you also have died to the law through the body of Christ, so that you may belong to another, to Him who has been raised from the dead, in order that we may bear fruit for God ... Now we are released from the law, having died to that which held us captive, so that we serve in the new way of the Spirit, and not in the old way of the written code" (Romans 7:4,6 ESV). We aren't obligated to serve by a cold list of regulations; we are free to serve in a new and Spirit-led way!

The Spirit will steer us as we move toward opportunities to serve. It is up to us to get going and watch for the cues we may see along the way.

SPIRITUAL NEEDS, SPIRITUAL SOLUTIONS

Most of us see our need for spiritual confidence in the area of ministry more than any other area. That can be a good thing. Spiritual needs often result in spiritual solutions if we are willing to take our needs to God.

"When you had daily troubles to take to the throne of grace, were you more spiritually alert than you are now? Easy roads make sleepy travelers."- C.H. Spurgeon

"Wisdom and philosophy never found out God; He makes Himself known to us through our needs."-J.N. Darby

"How much happier you would be if you only knew that these people cared nothing about you! How much larger your life would be if your self could become smaller in it; if you could really look at other men with curiosity and pleasure; if you could see them walking as they are in their sunny selfishness and virile indifference! You would begin to be interested in them you would break out of this tiny and tawdry theater in which your own little plot is always being played, and you would find yourself under a freer sky, in a street full of splendid strangers... How much happier you would be, how much more of you there would be, if the hammer of a higher God could smash your small cosmos, scattering the stars like spangles, and leave you in the open, free like other men to look up as well as down.[xlvii]

APPENDIX A

THE PROVIDENCE OF GOD

The Sovereign King of all.

(Rm. 11:33-34)

    a. God is the creator and therefore the owner of everything. "The earth is the Lord's, and all it contains, the world, and those who dwell in it." Ps. 24:1

    b. God does whatever He wants, contingent only upon Himself. "Our God is in the heavens; He does whatever He pleases." Ps. 115:3. "What [God's] soul desires, that He does." Job 23:13; Ps. 135:6; Isa. 46:9-10; Dan. 4:35.

GOD'S ACTIONS IN THE NATURAL WORLD:

    a. God is the Creator of all. "For there is but one God, the Father, from whom are all things, and we exist for Him; and one Lord, Jesus Christ, by whom are all things, and we exist through Him" 1 Cor. 8:6.

    b.   God sustains the natural world. Without God, everything would cease to exist. Christ is seen in Scripture as "upholding the universe by His word of power" Heb. 1:3, and "In Him all things hold together" Col. 1:17; Jer. 31:35; Job 34:10-15.

God invades human history to fulfill His plan =

    a.   Nations and the times and places people are born into (Acts 17:26)

    b.   Salvation

    c.   Gifting and placement into the Body of Christ (1 Cor. 12:11, 18)

    d.   Special calling (Israel, Edom, the twelve, Paul, the prophets, etc.)

    e.   Judgment/discipline

    f.   Miracles/healing

    g.   Special comfort and protection

    h.   Revelation

    i.   Creation of life and sustaining of that life, "knitting" us together in the womb, etc.

    j.   Time of death? "Taking us?" I'm not 100 percent sure with this one; but there is a verse in Job: "Since his days are determined, and the number of his months is with You, and You have appointed his limits that he cannot pass" (Job 14:5). This was said by Job, who was later commended by God – but it's not clear if he's saying God "takes" people at "their time," or if it's referring to a general "limit" that man can't pass. Or another possibility is that we do have a "death-date," but by our choices can "cut our own time short." Whatever the case, God is certainly able to prolong life or cut it short as seen with Hezekiah and Ananias and Sapphira.

i. Strange cases: Pharaoh (Rm. 9:15-18), Ananias and Sapphira

Discussion: How do these aspects of God's Providence give us spiritual confidence?

The Fallenness Factor.

a. The Natural World groans (Rm. 8:19-22)

b. Humanity's Consequences

c. Satan's role as kosmokrator

Problem #1 = Permitted Evil?

God and Satan.
Eph. 1:9-12 vs. 2 Thess. 2:9; Eph. 2:1-2; Mt. 24:24.
God = pantokrator Satan = kosmokrator.
"God neither causes sin, incites it, authorizes it, nor approves it. He does permit it by allowing His creatures, whom He has endowed with a moral will, to rebel against His authority. He then sovereignly overrules their evil to accomplish His predetermined purposes. In the allowance of evil, God demonstrates how great He really is." Tony Evans p.99
"It must be certain that evil, or at least the system of which evil is an inevitable part, will in the long run prove to be of greater good than the alternative would have been. For God, who knows all things and all possibilities, deemed even the consequences He would

experience, including the death of His Son, to be worth the total benefit." Erickson p.288-289.

Problem #2 = Determinism and free will?

"A man makes plans in his heart, but the Lord determines his steps" Prov. 16:9 (Prov. 19:21, 21:1; Rev. 17:17; Ps. 33:10-11)

a. hard determinism

b. libertarianism

c. soft determinism

(Above ideas taken from Scott R. Burson and Jerry L. Walls)

Problem #3 = "Foreknowledge" and ultimate power?

(1 Pet. 1:1-2; Rm. 8:29)

Conclusion: God is the owner and ruler of everything. He is all-knowing, all-powerful and completely free from limitation. These attributes dictate that He is Sovereign. God's Sovereignty is not a role He holds passively in heaven – He sustains the natural world and works actively in human history to accomplish His purpose. "Your choices will not determine whether God winds up where He wants to go. He will arrive at His destination ... either through you, around you, over you, by you, or in spite of you." Tony Evans p.92.

> "Nothing so invigorates our souls, so ravishes our hearts, so diminishes our anxieties, and so ennobles our existence as being supremely preoccupied with God's greatness and presence. This is what you and I were made for." –Dwight Edwards *Revolution Within*

HUMAN AGENCY

Freedom and responsibility

We can reject the will of God and His plan for our lives. Luke 7:30. Mt. 23:37; Mt. 7:21; Jn. 7:17; Acts 14:16

Obedience to God's commands

Why give commands and imperatives if we don't have free will in regards to God's will? 1 Thess. 4:3; 1 Thess. 5:17-19.

Accountability

Why are we held accountable if we are determined? Why are we rewarded for something we didn't really choose to do? There must be freedom and dignity if there is responsibility.

Evangelism and the Sovereignty of God

Are Christians elected by God?

a. God does not desire any to perish (2 Pet. 3:9-10; 1 Tim. 2:4; 1 Tim. 4:10; Jn. 12:32). However, God created humans foreknowing that they would suffer the judgment He deems necessary for that rejection. Therefore, isn't it true that it is God's will for some to perish? (Effectual or Permissive will vs. Moral will). We can say this: It is God's will for all persons to have a right relationship with Him. In this statement, we see that God desires all to come to salvation and that He desires that they make the choice to be in that relationship of their own volition.

b. Why does the Bible say that Christians are "chosen" or "predestined"? Does this mean that people are also "chosen" to go to hell?

    –   Predestined according to the foreknowledge of our choices.

      – Chosen for purposes as a servant (not for salvation). <Eph. 1; Lk. 9:35>. "We share in both the position of Christ beside God and the chosenness of Christ by God. The chosenness of Christ has, of course, nothing to do with going to heaven or hell. He is not chosen to go to heaven, but to be God's servant. The fact that He is chosen affects His function in God's plan." *God's Strategy in Human History.* P. 87-88.

  c. Catchers of men, willingness, "open doors," and our reason for being on earth.

CONCLUSIONS:

Everything that happens, happens because God permits it to happen (permissive will), however, not everything that happens is in accord with His ultimate desire (moral will). Choices that we make to accept or reject God's plan for us can change things in this world and the next because God has ordained to let our choices have consequences. If this were not the case, imperatives would be meaningless and so would verses about us being soldiers in a spiritual battle. Satan's freedom to choose and our freedom to choose would only be illusions.

1. How are we to live?

Why we must think rightly about God.

"The God most of us worship is too small. The God of most Christians seems anemic, weak, and limited. He does not have the capacity to make a difference, or turn things around. The God most of us serve resembles more the flickering of a candle than the burning of the noonday sun. One reason for this is that we do not understand God's sovereignty. We have allowed God to be everywhere but on His throne, and we have paid dearly in our own spiritual failure and weakness and limited power because the God we talk about has little to do with the sovereign God of the universe … Only when you understand that this is the kind of God with whom we have will you take seriously the issue of His authority. " Tony Evans. P. 89

Why we must take responsibility for our actions or lack thereof.

God created us as valuable image-bearers with true dignity, responsibility, and freedom. Our freedom can be used to reject or follow God's plan for our lives. God has allowed our choices to have true effect in this life and in the life to come. To believe that our choices have no real effect is to begin to make unhealthy presumptions upon God.

"The best argument for Christianity is Christians; their joy, their certainty, their completeness. But the strongest argument against Christianity is also Christians – when they are somber and joyless, when they are narrow and repressive, then Christianity dies a thousand deaths." – Sheldon Vanauken

2. The Mystery

This tension between God's sovereignty and human responsibility is a tension that cannot be fully understood or proven. Perhaps God wants this topic to remain a bit unclear to us. However, I think it's wise to bring up this element of mystery only after an honest look at the information we do have available to us.

APPENDIX B

TYPES OF ELECTION IN THE NEW TESTAMENT

1. **Of Christ:**
    Lk. 9:35, 23:35; 1 Pet. 2:4, 2:6; Isa. 42:1

2. **Of the Church in Christ:**
    Rom. 8:33 (16:13); Eph. 1:4; Col. 3:12; 1 Thess. 1:4; 2 Tim.
    2:10; Titus 1:1; 1 Pet. 1:2, 2:9, 5:13; 2 Pet. 1:10; Rev. 17:14
    (Mt. 24:22-31; Mark 13:20-27; [Luke 18:7?])

3. **Of the nation of Israel:**
    Acts 13:17; Rom. 9:11, 11:28; Isa. 45:4; Deut. 7:7

4. **Of believers in the nation of Israel:**
    Rm. 11:5, 7

5. **Of the twelve disciples:**
    Lk. 6:13; Jn. 6:70, 13:18, 15:16, 19; Acts 1:2, 24-25

6. **Of Paul:**
    Acts 9:15, 22:14; 1 Cor. 9:1, 15, etc.

*Above word study taken from *God's Strategy in Human History* p. 87

APPENDIX C

GOD'S PROMISES*

PRAYER

Rev. 3:20 – God initiates with us

Mt. 18:20 – God will be in our midst when we come together in prayer

Heb. 4:15-16 – God is sympathetic

Heb. 10:19-25 – God has cleansed our conscious and opened the way for us to approach Him freely

2 Thess. 3:5 – God can direct our hearts into His love

Rm. 8:26-27 – God gives help in prayer

Jn. 14:12-14 – Answered prayer

1 Jn. 5:14 – Answered prayer

2 Thess. 1:11-12, 3:3 – God will answer prayers and protect us from Satan

Phil. 3:15; Ps. 139:23-24 – God reveals our attitude to us in prayer

WORD

1 Cor. 2:16 – We have the mind of Christ

Jn. 15:26 – God's Spirit bears witness to us of Him

2 Tim. 1:7 – God gives us a spirit of "sound judgment" or "self-discipline"

Heb. 13:20-21 – God can equip us

2 Thess. 2:16-17 – God gives us comfort and strength

2 Cor. 10:3-5 – God has given us powerful weapons to battle the kosmos

Jas. 1:5 – God offers wisdom without reproach to anyone who asks

Isa. 55:10-11 – God's Word makes a difference to people when they hear it

1 Thess. 2:13 – God's Word performs its work in believers

SUFFERING/DISCIPLINE

Rm. 8:28 – God can work all things together for good

Heb. 12:7-11 – God disciplines His children, but a harvest can occur as a result (to those who have been trained by it)

2 Tim. 4:16-17 – God can stand with us and strengthen us

Rm. 15:5-18 – God gives perseverance, encouragement, joy, and peace

2 Cor. 12:9-10 – In our weakness, God is strong

Ps. 27:1-3 – God is our defense and our light

FELLOWSHIP

Mt. 16:18 – Hell will not overcome God's church

Rm. 16:20 – God will crush Satan under the feet of His church

2 Tim. 1:7 – God gives us a spirit of love

Rm. 15:5-18 – God gives us unity

Jer. 32:39 – God gives us a new heart of love

1 Thess. 4:9 – God teaches us to love one another

MINISTRY

Phil. 4:13 – We can do all things through God who gives us strength

Ps. 127:1 – God builds and watches

Acts 1:8 – God gives us power

1 Cor. 12:4-11 – God gives us gifting and roles in His Body

2 Cor. 2:14-3:6 – God manifests His aroma through us and makes us adequate ministers

Eph. 2:10 – God has prepared good works for us to do

Heb. 9:14 - God cleanses our consciences from dead works so we can serve Him

Jn. 15:4-5, 16 - God appoints and helps us to bear fruit

EVANGELISM

Jn. 12:32 – God draws all men to Himself

Jn. 16:8-11 – God convicts all men of sin, righteousness, and judgment

Acts 14:3 – God bears witness to the world of His grace, and can give the power to perform miracles

Jn. 6:44-45 – God draws and teaches men

Col. 4:3 – God can open doors for us

Eph. 6:19-20 – God gives us utterance

2 Cor. 2:14 – God manifests His aroma through us

DISCIPLE-MAKING

1 Cor. 3:5-7 – God gives opportunities and causes the growth in people

Mt. 28:18-20 – God is with us as we make disciples

LEADERSHIP

1 Tim. 1:12 – God strengthens us and appoints us to service

Acts 13:2, 4 – The Spirit can call and send us

Acts 20:28 – God makes people overseers

TEACHING

Isa. 55:10-11 – God's Word will have an effect on those who hear it

1 Thess. 2:13 – God's Word performs its work in Believers

Eph. 6:19-20 – God can give us utterance

1 Cor. 2:1-5, 12-13 – God can teach us to teach with spiritual words and spiritual thoughts in power

SERVING

Rm. 7:4, 6 – God enables us to serve in the newness of the Spirit

1 Thess. 4:9 – God teaches us to love one another

1 Cor. 16:9 – God can open a door for effective service

*This list is not exhaustive.

References

[i] Php. 3:3b

[ii] v. 12 and 18

[iii] Parrhesia is found in the following passages:
Confidence = (12x) Acts 2:29; Acts 26:26; Phm. 8-9; 1 Tim. 3:13; Acts 4:13; Acts 4:29; Heb. 10:19; Heb. 4:16; 1 Jn. 2:28; 1 Jn. 3:21; 1 Jn. 4:17-18; 1 Jn. 5:14.
Boldness = (10x) Acts 9:27-28; Eph. 3:12; Eph. 6:19-20; 2 Cor. 3:12; 1 Thess. 2:2; Acts 4:31; Acts 14:3; Acts 18:26; Acts 19:8; Phil. 1:20.
Delight/ Joyfulness = (5x) Isa. 55:2; Isa. 58:14; Isa. 66:11; Job. 27:10; Job 22:26.
State plainly = (4x) Jn. 10:24; Jn. 11:14; Jn. 16:25, 29; Mk. 8:32.
Openness = (3x) Acts 28:31; Jn. 7:13; Jn. 18:20.
Publically = (3x) Jn. 7:26; Jn. 11:54; Col. 2:15.
Fearlessness = (1x) Ps. 34:4.
Other Biblical words that convey the same idea for "confidence:"
Pepoithesis = Trust, Confidence
    2 Cor. 1:15, 3:4-6, 8:22, 10:2; Eph. 3:12; Phil. 3:4.
Hupostasis = Stand under, Foundation, Confidence, Constancy, Expectation, To stand.
    Heb. 1:3; 2 Cor. 9:4, 11:17; Heb. 3:14, 11:1.

[iv] see endnote 1 above

[v] "The Weight of Glory" C.S. Lewis

[vi] From his sermon "Pride and Humility" delivered at New Park Street Chapel, Southwark 1856

[vii] p.20

[viii] Exodus 4 and 1 Cor. 2

[ix] "The Marriage Builder" Larry Crabb p.75

[x] "The Marriage Builder" Larry Crabb p.75

[xi] "We Would See Jesus" Roy and Revel Hession pp.140-142

[xii] "The New Super Spirituality" Francis Schaeffer

[xiii] "A verse that may come to mind at this point is Isaiah 64:6 – "All our righteousness is as filthy rage." It is unfortunate that one often hears this verse quoted without any regard for context, and we must be careful here. Those in Isaiah who say "All of our righteousness is as filthy rage" go on in the next verse to accuse God of hiding His face from them. The latter is, we note, explicitly denied by God in Isaiah 65:1,2 where He says that he is not hiding but rather is offering Himself to them. (We might also compare Isaiah 63:17 with 65:12 where God affirms that it was not His doing but their own choice to reject His call and go against His wishes.) There is, then, no reason to suppose that the Lord endorses these people's extreme position over human sinfulness. It is not even a guard against spiritual pride, for God accuses these same people of a "holier than thou" attitude in 65:5. None of this is to deny that salvation is "not of works lest any man should boast," but it is to affirm that God's attitude to His servants' righteousness is different from that often supposed." – "God's Strategy in Human History" Roger T. Forster and V. Paul Marston. p. 14

[xiv] 1 Peter 4:8

[xv] "The Imitation of Christ" Thomas a Kempis

[xvi] Use search word "Accusation" to find the class notes or teacher's notes.

[xvii] "An Introduction to Systematic Theology" Cornelius Van Til

[xviii] 1 Cor. 7

[xix] "Green Letters" Miles Stanford. pp. 41-42

[xx] 2 Tim. 2:9, Mt. 24:25, Mt. 5:18, 1 Pet. 1:25, Ps. 119, Lk. 16:17, Ps. 29

[xxi] "Inspiration and Canonicity of the Scriptures" R. Laird Harris is one helpful book. There are others too; I really like the first section of Gleason Archer's "An Introduction to the Old Testament" for reading on this topic, and there is also a lot of good information in a much more accessible, succinct form on the Xenos website: www.xenos.org search words "canonicity" and "inspiration"

[xxii] "Orthodoxy" G.K. Chesterton. p.31-32

[xxiii] Eph. 6:12ff

[xxiv] "Life on the Highest Plane: God's Plan for Spiritual Maturity" Ruth Paxson. p.393

[xxv] "Prayer Power Unlimited" J. Oswald Sanders

[xxvi] "The Price of Power" J. Stuart Holden. pp.75-83

[xxvii] "Green Letters" Miles Stanford. P.10

[xxviii] "Green Letters" Miles Stanford. P.38

[xxix] "The Power of Prayer and the Prayer of Power" R.A. Torrey. P.70

[xxx] "Prayer: Rebelling Against the Status Quo" by David Wells

[xxxi] "The Path of Prayer" Samuel Chadwick

[xxxii] 2 Thess. 2:16-17; 2 Tim. 4:16-17; Rm. 15:5-18; 2 Cor. 12:9-10 just to name a few.

[xxxiii] "The Brothers Karamazov" Fyodor Dostoevsky

[xxxiv] v.25a, 28-29

[xxxv] Psalm 23:4, 27:1-3, Heb. 13:6, Prov. 3:25-26, Ps. 112:7, Isa. 35:4, Isa. 41:10, Rom. 8:15, 1 Jn. 4:17-18, etc.

[xxxvi] – J.H.T.

[xxxvii] "The Four Loves" C.S. Lewis

[xxxviii] 2 Corinthians 5:20-6:10

[xxxix] Rm. 8

[xl] 2 Timothy 1:7

[xli] Jn. 12:32; Jn. 16:8-11; Acts 14:3; Jn. 6:44-45

[xlii] Col. 4:3

[xliii] Eph. 6:19-20

[xliv] 2 Cor. 2:14

[xlv] www.xenos.org "Theology of Failure" by Dennis McCallum

[xlvi] "Spiritual Leadership" by J. Oswald Sanders, "Christian Leadership" by Bruce Powers, and "Effective Pastoring" by Bill Lawrence are a few that I really like.

[xlvii] "Orthodoxy" by G. K. Chesterton p.15